CONTINENTS

Antarctica

Leila Merrell Foster

Heinemann
LIBRARY

www.heinemann.co.uk/library
Visit our website to find out more information about Heinemann Library books.

To order:

 Phone ++44 (0)1865 888066

Send a fax to ++44 (0)1865 314091

Visit the Heinemann Bookshop at www.heinemann.co.uk/library to browse our catalogue and order online.

First published in Great Britain by Heinemann Library, Halley Court, Jordan Hill, Oxford OX2 8EJ, a division of Reed Educational and Professional Publishing Ltd. Heinemann is a registered trademark of Reed Educational and Professional Publishing Ltd.

OXFORD MELBOURNE AUCKLAND JOHANNESBURG BLANTYRE GABORONE IBADAN PORTSMOUTH NH (USA) CHICAGO

© Reed Educational and Professional Publishing Ltd 2002
The moral right of the proprietor has been asserted.

Designed by Depke Design
Originated by Dot Gradations
Printed by South China Printing in Hong Kong, China

06 05 04 03 02
10 9 8 7 6 5 4 3 2 1
ISBN 0 431 15794 4

British Library Cataloguing in Publication Data
Foster, Leila Merrell
    Antarctica. – (Continents)
    1.Antarctica – Juvenile literature
    I.Title
    919.8'9

Acknowledgements

The publishers are grateful to the following for permission to reproduce copyright material: Tony Stone/Ben Osborne, p. 4; Earth Scenes/David C. Fritts, p. 6; Tony Stone/Kim Heacox, p. 7; Peter Arnold/Gordon Wiltsie, pp. 8, 13; Tony Stone/Kim Westerskov, pp. 11, 17, 28; Photo Edit/Anna Zuckermann, p. 15; Photo Edit/Jack S. Grove, p. 16; Bruce Coleman/Fritz Polking, Inc., p. 20; Animals Animals/Johnny Johnson, p. 21; Earth Scenes/Stefano Nicolini, p. 22; Earth Scenes/Patti Murray, p. 23; Corbis/Bettmann Archive, p. 24; The Granger Collection, p. 25; Peter Arnold/Bruno P. Zehnder, p. 27; Earth Scenes/B. Herrod, p. 29.

Cover photo reproduced with permission of Science Photo Library/Tom Van Sant, Geosphere Project/Planetary Visions.

Our thanks to Jane Bingham for her assistance in the preparation of this book.

Every effort has been made to contact copyright holders of any material reproduced in this book. Any omissions will be rectified in subsequent printings if notice is given to the Publisher.

Contents

Some words are shown in bold, **like this**.
You can find out what they mean by looking in the glossary.

Where is Antarctica?

Snow-covered mountains in Antarctica

A continent is a vast mass of land that covers part of the Earth's surface. There are seven continents in the world, and Antarctica is the fifth largest. It is shaped almost like a circle with the **South Pole** at its centre. Antarctica lies below the **equator**, in the half of the world known as the **Southern Hemisphere**.

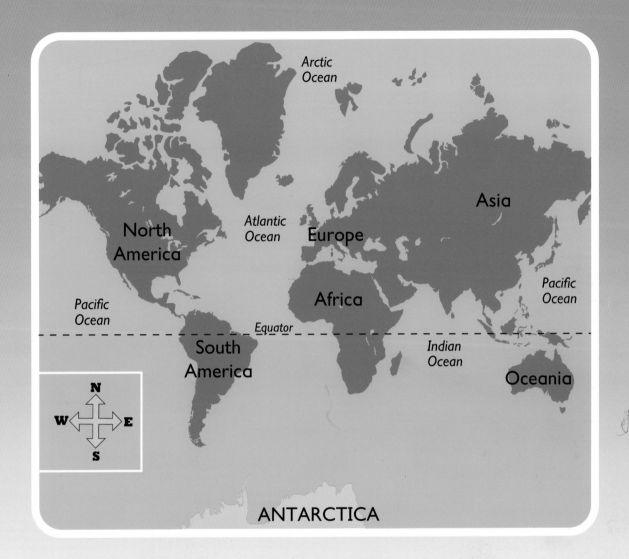

Antarctica is further away from the equator than any other continent. This means that it is very cold. The world's lowest temperature, of -89.2 °C, was recorded there. In central Antarctica, close to the South Pole, the Sun sets only once a year. It is dark for six months in winter and light for six months in summer.

Ice sheet

Mountains buried under ice

It is so cold in Antarctica that when the snow falls it does not melt. Instead, snow keeps on building up in layers. The weight of the snow on top presses down on the layers of snow below and forms ice. This solid sheet of ice covers nearly all the land in Antarctica. It is called the Antarctic **ice cap**.

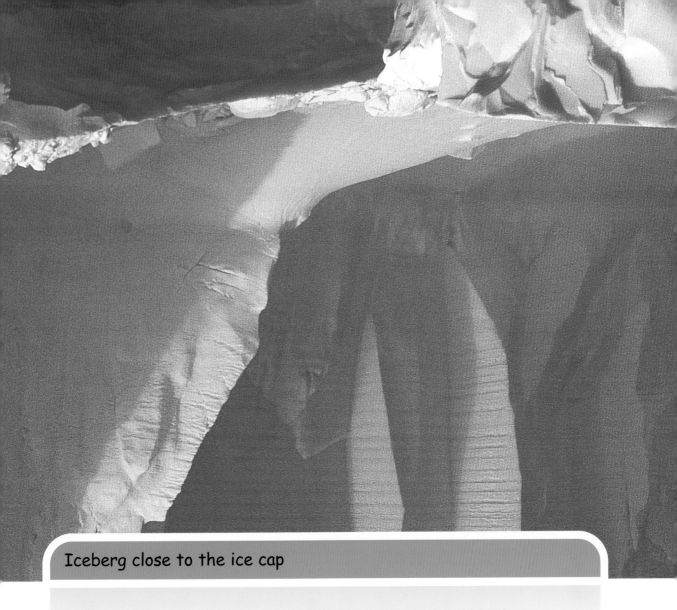

Iceberg close to the ice cap

The Antarctic ice cap is about two kilometres thick. It contains more than two thirds of all the fresh water in the world. If the ice cap ever melted, the level of the seas throughout the world would rise by 60 metres. All the towns and cities along the coasts would disappear underwater.

South Pole

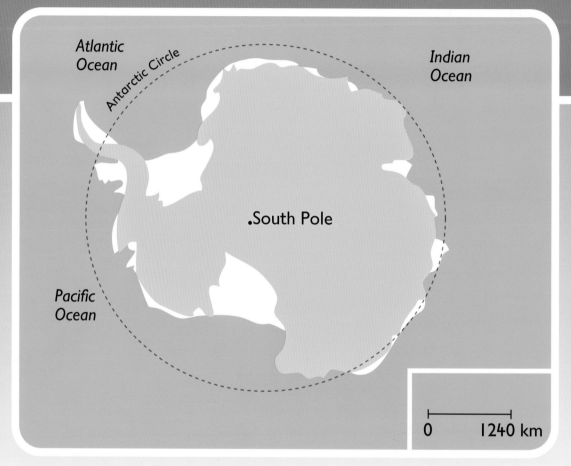

Atlantic
Ocean

Antarctic Circle

Indian
Ocean

.South Pole

Pacific
Ocean

0   1240 km

The **North Pole** in the Arctic and the **South Pole** in
Antarctica are the furthest places on Earth away from
the **equator**. If you drew a line between the two Poles,
it would run right through the centre of the Earth. This
imaginary line connecting the Poles is called the Earth's
axis. The Earth spins around on its axis.

Pole marking the South Pole

People have set up a real pole to mark the position of the South Pole. If you walked around that pole, you would be walking around the world! Surrounding the continent of Antarctica is an imaginary line called the Antarctic Circle. Almost all of Antarctica lies inside the Antarctic Circle.

Weather

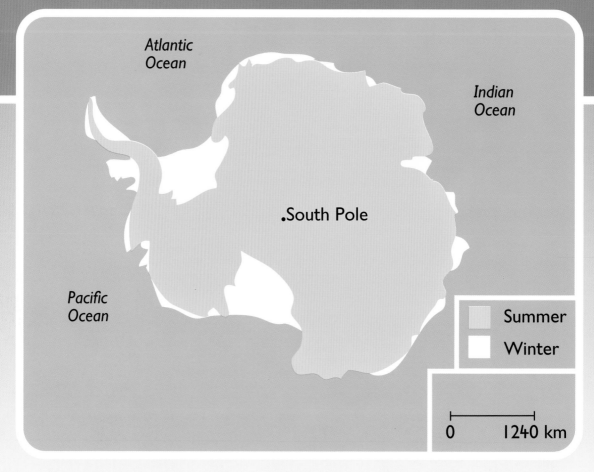

Atlantic
Ocean

Indian
Ocean

Pacific
Ocean

.South Pole

Summer

Winter

0   1240 km

The vast **ice cap** that covers Antarctica varies in size
between summer and winter. In the warmer summer
months, some of the ice at the edge of the ice cap melts.
In winter, the sea at the edge of the ice cap freezes
again. This frozen seawater is called pack ice.

Icy desert in central Antarctica

In the centre of Antarctica is an icy desert. Very little snow falls there, and winds whip up **blizzards** that can last for days. Antarctica is the coldest and windiest place on Earth. Even in summer, the temperature rarely rises above **freezing point**. The cold is so severe it can freeze human skin in 60 seconds.

Mountains

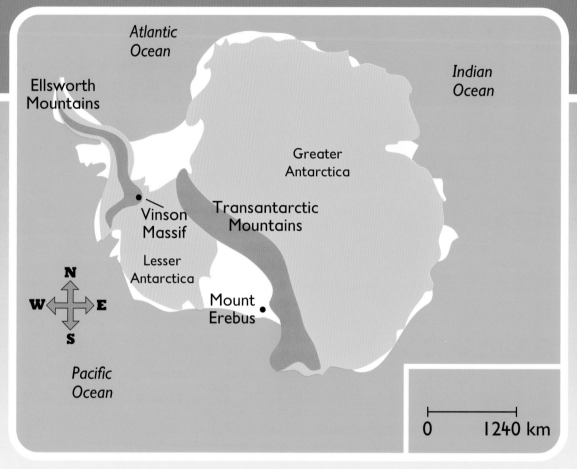

Atlantic
Ocean

Indian
Ocean

Ellsworth
Mountains

Greater
Antarctica

Vinson
Massif

Transantarctic
Mountains

Lesser
Antarctica

N
W **E**
S

Mount
Erebus

Pacific
Ocean

0   1240 km

The Transantarctic Mountains run right across Antarctica.
They divide the continent into two areas – Greater Antarctica
and Lesser Antarctica. To the east of the mountains, Greater
Antarctica rises in a massive dome of ice. To the west is
Lesser Antarctica. Scientists believe that Lesser Antarctica is
made up of three huge pieces of rock stuck together by ice.

The Vinson Massif in the Ellsworth mountains

The highest point in Antarctica is the Vinson **Massif**, which is 4897 metres high. It is in the Ellsworth mountain **range** in western Antarctica. In the south of the continent is Mount Erebus, an **active volcano**. Mount Erebus **erupts** at least once a day, throwing out small boulders.

 # Ice

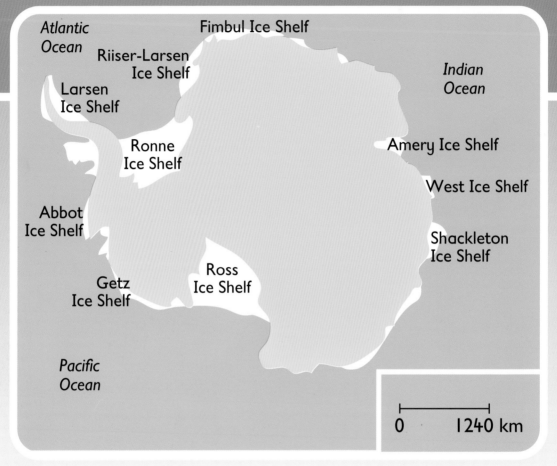

Atlantic
Ocean

Fimbul Ice Shelf

Riiser-Larsen
Ice Shelf

Indian
Ocean

Larsen
Ice Shelf

Ronne
Ice Shelf

Amery Ice Shelf

West Ice Shelf

Abbot
Ice Shelf

Shackleton
Ice Shelf

Getz
Ice Shelf

Ross
Ice Shelf

Pacific
Ocean

0   1240 km

Around the edges of Antarctica are huge slabs of ice that hang over the sea like shelves. Some of these **ice shelves** are enormous – the Ross Ice Shelf is the size of France. During the warmer summer months, chunks of ice break away from the ice shelves and form **icebergs**.

Icebergs can travel 13 kilometres in a day

Once they have broken away from the ice shelf, the icebergs are carried out to sea by strong **currents**. Icebergs are very dangerous for ships because they are much larger than they seem. Nine tenths of the ice floats below the water. Eventually, icebergs melt and crack apart, but this can take many years.

Glaciers

Glacier on the Antarctic coast

The continent of Antarctica is shaped like a dome. Ice is constantly being formed in the high centre of Antarctica. Very slowly, the ice slides outwards, down the slopes of the dome. These slow-moving rivers of ice are called **glaciers**. Eventually, the glaciers reach the edge of Antarctica.

Ice cliff at the edge of a glacier

Glaciers move incredibly slowly. The ice at the bottom of the glacier gets squashed by the ice above. Then the whole glacier slides forwards. Glaciers can look like huge cliffs of ice. The Lambert Glacier is the world's largest glacier. It is more than 400 kilometres long and 40 kilometres wide at the coast.

# Oceans and seas

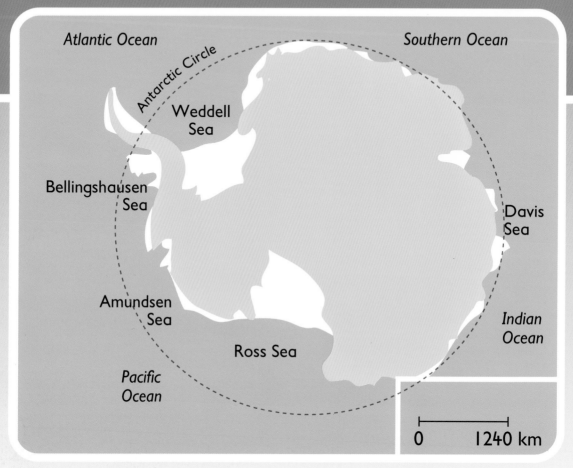

Atlantic Ocean

Southern Ocean

Antarctic Circle

Weddell
Sea

Bellingshausen
Sea

Davis
Sea

Amundsen
Sea

Indian
Ocean

Ross Sea

Pacific
Ocean

0   1240 km

Antarctica is surrounded by an icy cold area of sea
known as the Southern Ocean. Closer to land are several
small seas, such as the Weddell Sea. The Southern Ocean
stops the warmer water in the Atlantic, the Pacific and
the Indian Oceans from reaching the ice and melting it.

Stormy weather in the Southern Ocean

The Southern Ocean is famous for its strong **currents**, violent winds and monstrous waves. Most ships travelling to Antarctica leave from the Falklands Islands, at the tip of South America. The journey takes three days in calm weather but when it is stormy it can take several weeks.

Animals

Emperor penguins and their young

Sea birds, such as terns and petrels, visit Antarctica, but most of them fly north for the winter. One bird that stays in Antarctica all the year round is the penguin. Penguins have a thick layer of fat and soft, downy feathers to keep them warm. They are excellent swimmers and catch fish from the sea.

Elephant seals with a trunk-like 'nose'

For many years, people hunted the whales and seals that lived in Antarctica, but now there are laws to protect these animals. The seals of Antarctica spend most of their time hunting for fish in the icy seas, but they give birth to their babies on land. Most Antarctic whales eat tiny sea creatures called krill.

Plants

Lichen growing on rocks

Lichen is the most common plant in Antarctica. It grows on rocks and needs very little water to survive. Some types of moss also grow in Antarctica. Moss and lichen grow very slowly. Scientists think that some of the moss and lichen plants in Antarctica are more than a thousand years old.

Tussock grass in northern Antarctica

No trees grow in Antarctica, and only two types of flowering plant have ever been found there. The only grass that grows in Antarctica is called tussock grass. It is found in the northernmost part of the continent, where it is warmest. Tussock grass has very strong roots to stop it being blown away.

Explorers

The Endurance trapped in ice

Early explorers sailed to Antarctica in wooden ships. But the strong, sharp ice easily tore apart their boats. This photograph shows the *Endurance*, the ship of the British explorer Ernest Shackleton. Shackleton and his crew had to escape from their ship in lifeboats. Some of them drifted for five months before they reached land.

The Norwegian explorer Roald Amundsen

The first person to reach the **South Pole** was Roald Amundsen. He arrived at the Pole in 1911. Amundsen and his team used sleds pulled by dogs to carry their equipment. A British explorer, Robert Scott, used ponies to pull his sleds. He reached the South Pole in 1912, but he died on the journey home.

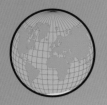 # All the countries

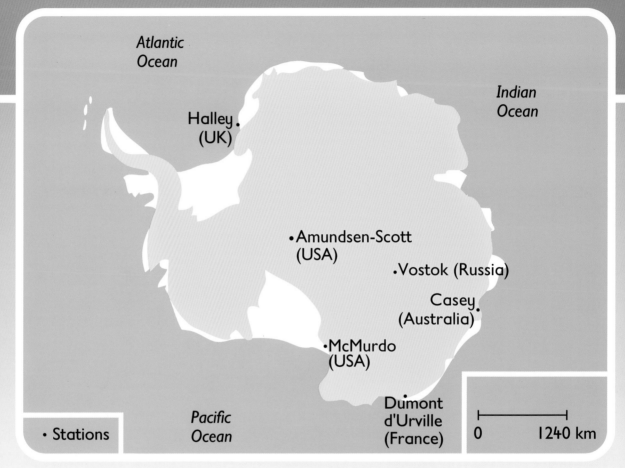

Antarctica is the only continent with no countries, but many countries have **research stations** there. Scientists from over fifteen different nations live in the stations and do experiments on the ice. The map shows some of the main stations in Antarctica and the countries that set them up.

McMurdo station in southern Antarctica

In 1959, 12 countries signed an agreement to keep Antarctica free for peaceful research. Another agreement was signed in 1991 to stop all **mining** in the Antarctic. During the summer, small groups of tourists visit Antarctica. They are carefully controlled to make sure they do not leave any rubbish.

Science

Scientists using a weather balloon

Teams of scientists study the weather in Antarctica.
This helps them to understand more about weather all
over the world. They use **weather balloons** to test the
gases in the air. They also measure how much ice melts
in summer. They have discovered that more ice melts
each year and the world's weather is getting warmer.

Setting up equipment on the ice

Some scientists drill into the ice to find out what the weather was like hundreds of years ago. By measuring the layers of ice, they can see how much snow has fallen each winter. Other scientists in Antarctica study animals and plants, and some use powerful telescopes to look at the stars.

Fast Facts

1. Antarctica is the driest, highest and windiest place on Earth.

2. At its thickest point, the ice covering Antarctica is almost 5 kilometres deep.

3. The coldest temperature ever recorded was at Vostok Research Station in 1983. It was −89.2°C.

4. No rain falls on the land in Antarctica. It only rains around the edge of the coast.

5. Antarctica contains 70 per cent of the world's fresh water in the form of ice.

6. The biggest iceberg ever seen was larger than Belgium. It covered about 30,000 square kilometres.

7. Scientists have found fossils in Antarctica. This means that the continent was once warm and trees and other plants lived there.

8. Winds in the Southern Ocean around Antarctica can reach speeds of 300 kilometres an hour.

Glossary

active volcano hole in the earth from which hot, melted rock is thrown out

axis imaginary line through the middle of an object

blizzard heavy snowstorm

current movement of water

equator imaginary circle around the exact middle of the Earth

erupt to throw out rocks and hot ash

freezing point 0°C – the temperature at which water freezes

glacier very large mass of slow-moving ice and snow

iceberg large piece of ice that is floating in the sea

ice cap very thick layer of ice that covers a large area of land

ice shelf ice that sticks out from land over water

massif mountain peak

mining digging up things from under the Earth's surface

North Pole most northern spot on the Earth

range line of connected mountains

research station place where scientists work

Southern Hemisphere half of the Earth south of the equator

South Pole most southern spot on the Earth

weather balloons balloons used by scientists to measure weather

More books to read

What are Glaciers?, Claire Llewellyn, Heinemann Library, 2000

From the Arctic to the Antarctic, Rod Theodorou, Heinemann Library, 2000

My Best Book of Polar Animals, Christine Gunzi, Kingfisher, 2002

Index